GIVING THEM THEIR FLOWERS

STORIES OF LOVE

RANDI COLEY

To the people who came before me.
To my mentors , teachers and teachers: CH, AD and DE.
To   my   mother Beverly for raising me.

For my grandmothers Lois Swinney and Cordelia Kizer that were my friends,
and stern examples of womanhood.

To my daughters Jordan and Toriann.

For Jesse Hoover, the first man to tell me and show me what being valued and
loved was. I miss you.

To Isadore Kizer, my father.
I miss you, old man.

INTRODUCTION

A variety of anecdotal short stories and poetry with life lessons, and salutes to those that have affected me over the course of my 50 plus years of life. That impact may have been knowledge, taught me a skill or even gut-checked me. I have written about it and thanked them for this work. Gospel singer James Cleveland sang the song "Give Me My Flowers". I can't sing, so here is my offing. The words from the pen of a ready writer. Psalms 45:1.

A variety of poetry and short stories with salutes to those that I love.

That impact may have been knowledge, taught me a skill, or even gut-checked me.

I've written about our experiences and in every word thanked them.

We are family—Sister Sledge. I can't sing, so here is my offing.

The words from the pen of a ready writer.

Psalms 45:1.

MRS. PAISE

I didn't understand why I was the one. I would head down the street to sit with her.

It was afternoon, maybe early evening. She was sitting at the table. She could hear me approaching.

I didn't quite understand she was visually impaired. Diabetes snatched her vision and part of her legs.

Her heart was broken, her husband unfaithful. This little girl learned life lessons at her table. It not what you see but what you feel.

OLD MAN

*H*ow can I say the things that mean so much.

There was no one like him, he was one of a kind. No one could not tell him he wasn't fine.

It was always my dream, and I chased him.

The father, friend and dad I wanted. It was not to be. He wasn't perfect but he belonged to me.

It came to an end, June 23rd, 2022.
Alright, old man. I miss you.
Isadore Kizer Jr.

CAROLYN HALL

I was a little girl whose hair had to be cut, and I met a beautiful woman with an Afro.

Our team's Pom Pom coach. Too young to realize there was a baby on the way, she became Rahn Marie.

I asked questions, stayed in touch and learned a lot from a grown-up who treated me as a friend.

Never sharing too much, but enough to allow me to be child, and significant.

I will always be grateful, always love you. Most of all because you let me be a friend and a "kid".

TO JESSE

The first man to value me.
He called me his daughter.
It's funny how many believe blood makes you family.

When it's life that does, no matter what.

I think about all the pushes and pull ups you gave.
No one said I could but you made it possible, so I did.
I knew you had to go, and you left me alone.

The man that I first knew as dad.
In my life from 1985-1998, I miss you and take you with me always.
Jesse Hover

ANN DAVIS 6th Grade

*S*tately beauty sharply dressed.
    She kept her head up, instructing us.

We learned about reading, writing and arithmetic. Sprinkled with life lessons and some common sense.

Walking the rows, inspiring those who someday hoped to make a difference.

We learned about politics, economics and something's I can't remember.

But, in that foundation are memories galore. Sometimes now when I am out and about, I see her and grab a hug.

Thank you AD.

LOVING TO WRITE

*I*t was a contest.
A tall tale, exaggerated story.

I wrote about a woman that had a series of multiple births in a very short time.

It was funny, some thought it cute. Who would have know that now it is true.

I won the contest, took the prize.
The teacher smiled and asked to keep that
work.

What happens now is, I love to write.
Dedicated to Mrs. Skala-5th Grade

A LETTER TO MY YOUNGER SELF: THE CHILD THAT LIVES WITHIN

Little girl, little girl ... remember you are always a twin.

You're an individual, sharp, beautiful, and intelligent.

Keep your own personality.
Know you're beautiful when others look superficially.

Looks matter to some, while others value intellect and integrity.

Your value to some, will be your personality.
You must value yourself to maintain your dignity.

Hold on to your "no".
Don't let it go.

When the boys come talking down to you,
Understand, it's not you.

It's their issues that gaslight, manipulate, and victimize.
It's the lies, you've been fed your entire life.

You're more than enough.

Live in peace.

KINDERGARTEN

First day of school.
    I was so afraid.
My mom walked me in, my hand in hers.
A beautiful woman turned around, and I saw a new friend.
She was dressed in a white blouse and a black skirt.
She wore her hair in a bun.
A shiny belt adorned her waist.
I don't remember if she had on heels or not, but I remember the smile that was spread across her face.
She stepped forward and introduced herself, meeting my gaze.
I clung to my mom, trying not to let her hand go.
It's my new friend that promises we'll have fun.
I can trust her.
Anxiety didn't let me talk for the first few weeks.
Every day, she coaxed me to play, not requiring a word. Eventually, I spoke and joined the rest of the class.

Dedicated to Mrs. Smith.

HOPE

*W*hen you come from an abusive relationship or grew up abused, it can make you jaded.

At a young age I was molested and throughout most of my youth.

Several people took their turns until I was an adult. This abuse wasn't constant, it happened at various times.

One of the first things that abused people learn is to lie.
We're groomed how to do this from the first touch.

Abusers tell us to keep their "secrets", so others don't know the real monsters they are.

When the abuser hurts us and tells us to keep their secrets, it kills a piece of hope in us day by day.

We lie and hide, and in exchange they steal our hope.

As infants we're taught to hope when our parents take care of us, filled with love and without drama.

We exercise hope as we move through everyday life.
We hope to get that object we wait for all year.
We hope that our friends are truly friends as we get older.
We hope in the future as we plan our lives.

The time is now to take our hope back.
Hope is the very thing that gave us a reason to leave our abusers and start our life over in the face of many obstacles.
Hope for a brighter, violence free future for our children.
Hope makes us get out of bed and believe in the power of GOD.
Hope keeps your attitude positive and gives you the promise of another day.
Hope is the greatest gift when you have nothing else.
Don't give up.
Have hope.
Hold onto hope, and believe in it.
It's your help and will guide you even when others tell you all hope is lost.
Hope is the positive thinking that causes you to know every day has unlimited possibilities.
It allows you to face life over and again when the odds are against you.
Have hope, no matter what it looks like.
Have a positive attitude—it goes along with hope.

Be strong in your convictions.
Know that resisting temptation and side-stepping the traps of life will strengthen you.
Love helps you.

DEAL WITH IT

I'm not beautiful to be a darker skinned woman.
I don't have a pretty face to be a big girl.
I'm not surprisingly intelligent in spite of what I've overcome.

I am. A dark, intelligent, big, beautiful woman.
I am enough.
Deal with it!

MOTHERS...

$\mathcal{T}$here are women that give birth.

That's their contribution to the world.

They don't have any investment in the children they've brought forth.

Those children grow up and aren't given any guidance.

Some children are abused, neglected, or both.

Some have even died.

Although, technically called a mother they're simply women that have given birth.

I'm a mother...

I wake up with my children on my mind and fall asleep the same.

The sacrifices I've made are part of the territory and I don't mind.

I don't take vacations, sleep late, or forget who I am.

I'm a mother.

I buy clothes and food, cook, clean, provide shelter, give hugs and love.

I pray and cry. I yell and whisper.

I congratulate and reprimand.
I'm a mother.

Some would say this is a life sentence—eighteen years to life.
I've used the reference as well.
However, what "real" mother doesn't rush to get there when she is called or help her child in times of trouble?
Whether it's through prayer, finances, or consolation no matter their age.

I'm a mother.
It can be hard. The sleepless nights. The terrible two's. Those rough adolescent years of change or young adulthood when all parents are dumb and don't know anything.

I'm a mother through it all and for the rest of my life.

AN ODE TO MOTHERS

Conception...
        It was me, her, him, or them.
Labor... oh the pain!
Delivery... a child comes forth.

Tears of joy, pain, horror and even love...
Here you came.
There you go.
Breathe... life.
No breathe... death.

Being there for you.
Caring for you.
Feeding you.
Holding you.
Loving you.
Nurturing you.
Supporting you.

Late, long nights; colds, fever, and flu.

Through chicken pox and sore throats
She was there for you.
Each new step, or stumbling block, she was there to pick you up.

A mother has your back, even through the mess ups.
She's there for you.
You have her heart, she loves you.
She strengthens your mind; she reads to you in the womb. She cultivates the building of knowledge for the rest of your life.
She builds up your spirit.
She uplifts your soul to know who the Almighty GOD is. She teaches you to reverence Him and to know He is GOD.

A mother does all that GOD assigned her to do and more. She may have rough days, and some long nights but she accepts this because she knows she was called to be...
A Mother.
She accepted her charge and embraced it wholly.

That's what a mother is and was for me.
An ode to a mother, my mother...Beverly C, and her mother Lois B. Swinney, the matriarch of my family.

Lois B. Swinney May 1920- March 2014

MAMA

*B*eautiful and stately.
    I didn't think I looked like her.
She has long fingers with manicured nails.
Baby fine hair that she kept relaxed.
She was missing for a week—
No, she didn't run away nor was she taken.
She was in the hospital having surgery.
I missed her.
I cried for days asking, "Where is Mama?"
She held onto us, single because of divorce.
She worked hard and bought a house.
She kept us together by sacrifice and circumstance.
There's no one like her, she is one of a kind.
Not perfect, but she is mine.
I love my Mama.

GRANDMOTHER CHRONICLES

*P*salm 30:5
"Weeping may endure for a night, but joy cometh in the morning."

Yesterday morning as I played with my grandchildren, I taught them the part of the scripture printed above.

My baby girl's name is Joia.

So when I said, "Weeping may endure for a night, but Joy(-a) comes in the morning."

I touched her nose.

She laughed out loud and grabbed my cheeks.

Before, we went out for the day, they were quoting the scripture back at me.

Training them up!

They invoke some joy for me.

RANDI COLEY

GROWING OLD

*T*here's something to be said about growing old gracefully...
    I appreciate the slow slope of aging—remember it's been denied to many.
Some get better, finer, and more refined through the walk of time.
These bodies change going along with wrinkles and greying hair.

The vivacious curve of the breast seems to become a lump of sagging flesh.
Why get a breast lift? They fell because of the milk that fed your babies, weighting them, then depleting them.

Why get that tummy tuck and laser treatment?
To rid yourself of those beautiful stretch marks and round belly that carried the lives of those that not only grew in your body and continue to tug at the heart is almost blasphemy.

I know it looks like a basketball sometimes, Man.
Those tight abs and strong cut arms may have lessened and in exchange you gained wisdom by the muscles of your brain, not through the sweat of brawn.

Don't you see? Those few pounds and greying temples make you look distinguished and wise.

Your hair may be thinning or have left you bald.
You still look like the boy that love's heart knew.
You can't believe someone's heart still skips a beat.
Who they see is the young man, woman, or friend they've always known.

If all you see, or ever saw, was the outward appearance and have not yet measured the heart, spirit, and soul of the person you say you love, is it love?

What if that thing you felt changes? Or they can't make you feel the same physically? What if they become ill as people sometimes do? What if you had to care for them? Could you do it with kindness, tenderness, and love?

Do you really love them?

FREEDOM

*S*o many terms mean "liberty."

Movement without hinderance.

Complete and simple peace.

Freedom…

Deeds without judgment.

Joy unspeakable.

Emotion unencumbered.

The arms of love wrapped around.

Love brings freedom, and freedom grows in love.

LET GO AND BE FREE

*I*n the movie Shaka Zulu, he asked a question of a British Colonial Military man who had befriended him, "How do you catch a monkey?"

He didn't ask as one who didn't know—he was letting the man know that he was aware they had set him in a trap. Here it is...

How do you catch a monkey?

You take a clear long-necked jar and put something shiny inside.

The monkey will reach into the vessel, closing his fist on the object, therefore unable to pull out its hand and becoming trapped.

The monkey only has to open his hand to be free.

But he doesn't open his hand and ends up in captivity.

My question is, aren't we supposed to be smarter than monkeys?

Why do we allow ourselves to be trapped by ways, people, places, and things?

What shiny thing is holding you hostage?

Isn't it the time to let go of it all?

Let go and be free.

. . .

SOLDIER

*H*ey you over there...
Are you ready?
Are you standing in the gap? Are you awaiting your orders? Do you hear the call to arms?

Soldier, are you prepared? Are you preparing?
Be sober and vigilant.
Are you watching?

Warfare is not pretty. Blood has been shed. Lives have been lost. Scrimmages are fought every day.

Get up! Let's go!
Grab your shield.
Hold fast to your faith.
Run this race 'til the battle ends.

Be the strong soldier and when the battle is over...
You will win!

I PRESS ON

I haven't felt like myself lately...
        I press on.
I haven't been singing on key...
I press on.
May not have said that I love you and I care...
I press on.
I know I haven't reached out...
I press on.
It hasn't been easy to smile when I felt like crying...
I press on.
I haven't hugged you or even said hi...
Still, I press on.
I continue to strive in this walk with GOD, even when I see myself not being like He wants.
Even when I don't feel like it matters, I pray.
I pray for you, and as GOD has instructed me to ...
I love you.
Even when I don't like you.
No matter what may come, in spite of what may come
...I press on.

I CAN'T

I

understand disappointment. I've taken a lot of losses. I'm used to it. So don't tell me all about how it gets better.
I can't...
I remember being invisible as a teenager, abused, talked about and bullied. I remember standing for things no one else believed and being treated badly for it.
I can't...
Being called "ugly", "black" or told if you did or were like...you would be better. Or, that you should and blah, blah, blah.
I can't...
When you have been invisible so long, you don't expect anyone to see you, to care. It gets easy to keep going, you no longer expect love.
I can't...
And, it doesn't matter anymore that it hurts so bad it's a literal physical pain. Hope hurts like a knife to the heart. I feel the blood running cold.
I can't...
Because, I know God is good and he has blessed me beyond measure. But today...I can't let go, or give up hope. It's my nature and failure is not an option! I just need a pinch, the size of a seed. Faith won't let me, I can't let go!!!

THE DAMAGING EFFECTS OF LONELINESS AND THE POWERFUL PRECIOUS GIFT OF LOVE

*L*oneliness ...

It's a condition of the mind and body.

It can burden your thinking, your mood, and steal your appetite.

Loneliness can steal time.

You can lose a day, a month, a year, a decade.

Loneliness cannot be stopped, but you can choose how to deal with it.

Love ...

It's a gift from GOD, sustenance to the heart and soul.

It will uplift your thoughts, positively change your mood.

It will usher in unspeakable joy, balance your appetite, and fill your days with the wholeness that only GOD's love can give.

REFINEMENT TOPIC: LONELINESS

This morning the topic of Loneliness came to me. Loneliness is a part of the human condition—everyone experiences it.

Speaking as a natural woman, I don't get lonely often. However, when it happens, I've spent months or years without any emotional connection.

I'm not talking about a romantic partner either.

I'm talking about feeling disconnected from people.

I can be alone for long periods of time.

As I've learned to, I can even go without being touched.

My faith and hope in GOD keep me grounded.

Last night, I had the most amazing experience.

My granddaughter climbed on me and wrapped her arms around me. The embrace was simple, but it brought tears to my eyes.

It felt like love.

It gave me joy and met a need I hadn't thought about. Sometimes I need to experience the touch of another.

I'm thankful for the simplicity of it.

I felt like I had touched the hem of his garment.

I felt whole.

. . .

FRIENDSHIP

*F*riendship can best be described as a rose.

Soft and precious at a glance.

But when tested, engulfed by fury, can prove to be very strong.

Shaken and tossed, yet still a bud may grow.

A friendship like a rose can grow from almost nothing,

and blossom into something beautiful and as brilliant as a magnificent red rose.

SUNSHINE

My friend and confident.
Met by chance.
A need of sorts.
Confidential information and exchanges in due course.
Compassion met hope, and friendship was forged.
2003-2020.
I can't believe she suddenly left me.

Dedicated to Billie J. Lucious

FORTUNATE

O n her way home after a long day at work, she stopped at a gas station just off the highway to fill up.

She paid and returned to the car to pump the gas.

While pumping the gas, a man she had walked by as she came out of the station, who also happened to hold the door for her said, "Excuse me can I pump that for you?"

She was tired and cranky and didn't bother to look up or even make eye contact.

She simply said, "No thank you."

He stood there and asked, "Can we exchange information and possibly get to know one another?"

She backed up and said, "No."

When he asked why, she looked him in the eye and said, "I'm in love with some one and my heart belongs to him."

He looked away and said, "He's a fortunate man."

She smiled and replied, "I'm the fortunate one. In fact, I'm blessed. My love and heart belong to the Lord and Savior Jesus Christ. Do you know him?"

He smiled again and with a hint of sarcasm said, "I did."

"You can know him again," the woman contested.

He shook his head, and at the same time he bowed his head "I know."

Before he could move away, she asked, "Can we pray?"

He said, "Yes." The man accepted Christ back into his life that day.

"You're fortunate, too," she beamed.

He smiled as she walked away.

She pulled off from the gas station and thanked GOD for a renewed soul and being a fortunate woman who loved the Lord enough to share Him with someone else.

HURT

*T*his hurts...

I keep asking the question, but I know it was me, I did this.
I know this can't be fixed.
Where are you? I need you to speak.
I hurt every day because of your situation.
I was sorrowful knowing it was me.
 I brought you to this point, and it hurts.

I desire to reach out to you; I need to fix it.
I want to console you.
If I could barter for your relief and give you peace, I would.
I know.
It was ... me.
I did this.
I pray you have not set your heart, that GOD would soften it.
Don't walk away.
Please give love another chance.
GOD is always here.
GOD's arms of love are still reaching out to you.

The still small voice is beckoning for you.
Please come home.
Don't let go.
I hurt and it's for you.

TODAY

Someone rubbed their legs and complained that they hurt.

Another can't walk.

Another has no legs.

Someone cried, "I don't get paid enough." Another lost their job.

One said, "My place needs more."

Someone has no place to call home.

Someone said, "My heart aches."

Another's stop beating and their life is over.

Remember...what you're facing may be uncomfortable, it may even be hard, but someone else is facing far more or worse.

The grace of GOD is sufficient.

Be encouraged.

GOD has not forgotten you.

BECAUSE IT'S YOUR WILL LORD

Because it is your will Lord...
> I will give.
I will be kind.
I will love.
I will obey your word.
I will make my sacrifice, dedicated to you.
I will submit my body.
I will set apart my life for you.
Nevertheless, not my will Lord.
Your will be done.

I LOVE YOU ON PURPOSE

I love you on purpose.

Not because it's politically correct.
Not because of wealth or for fame.
But because you are you and you are just right for me.

When you love someone on purpose, it means you've made a conscious effort to freely offer the purest part of yourself.

That's what you got from me because I love you.

I want you to know...
I love you on purpose.

THE HEART

Thump, thump, thump...
It sounds like a rhythm.
It beats like drum.
Thump, thump, thump...
It carries blood, it carries love.
Thump, thump, thump...
Life, love, joy, pain, it carries us.
Thump, thump, thump...
It can only be heard through a stethoscope, an ear close to the breast, or by GOD.
Thump, thump, thump...
It holds hope, freely offers love, and is sometimes used as an object of pain.
GOD knows the heart.
Jesus accepted the call and massages it thoroughly.
When His love moved
Hearts were changed.
Now, love can flow and work.
Love cannot be moved.

YOU

*Y*ou smiled.
     I lowered my eyes and stepped to the side.
     I didn't want to appear desperate.
You spoke.
I nodded.
I didn't want to make others think I was flirting.
I found myself looking for you in every crowded room.
There you were.
I could hear your voice when everyone around us was speaking.
You give me joy.
I smile at the thought of you.
You cause my heart to skip a beat.

AIN'T SHE SWEET

*B*rown eyes and about six feet
      Not twenty-five, but nice and neat.
Met at the window,
She waved her hand.
Nah, man. I'll pay.
We *are* friends.

Was that a reflex or a grab for her hand?

Light talk and laughter
Warm smiles and hand holding.
A run to the theater for a movie—American Fiction.

It was an easy to slip into a routine.
It got really familiar, almost obscene.
Not intimate, but comfortable.
Fear is real and convictions stand.

It's definitely best to stay only friends.

IS IT LOVE?

I want to say hello.

I feel the need to apologize for standing aloof when I should have enveloped you in my arms.

But I will wait on GOD, and you until the change comes. GOD promised and he will bring it to pass.

Is it love?

Yes it is.

And, when it's real love, it's worth the wait.

Love will make you wait.

AN ODE TO LONGEVITY IN MARRIAGE

*H*ave you ever wondered what draws two people's hearts together?

What causes them to want to spend the rest of this life together?

How some seem like odd couples and others seem to fit together like a hand in glove.

When I look at them, I'm reminded of my grandmothers when they spoke of how they loved my grandfathers.

Superficial and material things don't last or compare with real and true love.

There is one thing I would like for those who get married—that you both have the foundation of salvation. He ought to be a man who truly loves GOD first and he is given to the woman of GOD *by* GOD.

If these things are present first, love will grow between the two people, and they will be together until the end of their lives.

Just as both sets of my grandparents did.

FOR THE LOVE OF MY HUSBAND

A special feeling, one we want to share.
    A need for understanding,
The hope someone will be there.
At rest on my pillow at night, I do understand.
My love is for you, and oh how you care.
I can't express to you, how I truly feel.
You could never really understand, thus my dreams seem unreal.
I've loved you since the day we met,
    our marriage seemed so right.
The moment since the first kiss was all we needed to make it that first night.
We held each other in the hope that this was all we needed, but the sun arose, and a new day came.
As did our troubles anew.
We've got to try so our love doesn't die.
Times have been hard and very tough.
But, if we try and love hard enough, we can make this marriage work.
I can recall that very first kiss, the way we held each other tight.
Remember all those pleasures that night?

Holding and kissing and knowing this was right ...
Can it be that way again after all the strife?
I'll be there to help you again as I did before—
My shoulder, your rock, when you shed a tear...
My love, your strength, when your filled with fear.
My darling when you call, be it far or near,
I'll always be there as I am right here.
For your love I know—no pain, no gain.
I'll be with you to weather the storm with the guidance of our LORD.
I can only pray on that faith-filled day,
our love is enough to help our marriage grow.
From this day on I promise my heart, my love, my soul.
To you, my dear, because I love you.

From a heart of hope
written R. Coley January 1989

HOLINESS IS THE TREE OF LIFE

*R*ooted in GOD's word.
      The trunk of salvation.
With branches of praises, prayers, and studying.
Leaves of hope, love, peace, and joy.
Seeds of testimony fill the ground.
For the one that planted, sprinkled with water from various souls.
GOD's increase is in the full-grown tree.

SAVING GRACE

On bended knee.
        Hands lifted in surrender.
Confession is made.

Words to live by—Wonderful Savior

Jesus Christ the Son of GOD.
Sacrificial Lamb for all men.
He is …
My Saving Grace.

LOVING TO WRITE

*I*t was a contest.
A tall tale, an exaggerated story.
I wrote about a woman who had multiple births in a very short time.
It was funny, some thought it cute.
Who would've known that now it's true.
I won the contest; I took the prize.
The teacher smiled and asked to keep that work.

What happens now is …
I love to write.

I Owe You an Apology...

It was a Friday night some years ago. You were standing in my line of sight. When you moved I thought...there he is.

You were smiling. I was preoccupied. Riding with someone who was ready to go, my "play daughter" who is in the wrong and I am purposely ignoring is flagging me to get my attention. Plus someone had just insulted me and gotten on my nerves. You got hit by the debris.

You did a spin, smiled and said Hello. I'd made up my mind to never get tied up with any man, in the wrong way ever again. I didn't trust myself, I smiled greeted you and side stepped away.

Although, I wanted to I didn't turn around. I said in my mind...."if it be God's will, this chance if it's real will come back again someday". That was my hope. But, I hurt you that day. That was not my intention.

I saw you with your head down, uncomfortable in my presence and sometimes just a look of questioning. There were many times I want to entreat you but instead I circle wide around you. Not, wanting to entice my flesh or try to provoke yours. I wanted to be sure this is really God, I have messed up so many times. This has got to be done right! You were never forgotten. Never far from my thoughts and heart. Gid's love has been working all the time, even then.

My looks/ facial expressions have nothing to do with you. It's posture, not wanting to let anyone that could hurt me in. Or, even to get close.

But God's love has pierced through my hurt and his love has touched my soul. A Sunday not to many days ago you I watched walk down the street. I wanted to pull over get out and tell you this. I simply want to start with it and build from there if it is not to late.

I know I missed it, that precious opportunity and you. Did I hurt you, am I to late??? Can I tell you now how much I have come to appreciate the very thought of you. Your manfuliness.

Your praises are beautiful to me and it erupts a passion and love in God, I have never known. Am I saying to much? Well let me stop and simply say...

I hurt you and I am sorry

ABOUT THE AUTHOR

Randi Coley born the last year of the 60's. Educated with a Bachelor's in Psychology and Maters of Health Science in Addictions studies. She is an addiction and mental counselor that has worked in the helping and social services field for 20 years. She is an entrepreneur with 2 community outreach organizations. Her goal through various forms of media is to educate, inspire, motivate, and uplift by words of inspiration, mentoring, leadership and behavioral modification practices for change.

Randi can be found on Social Media at the below locations…
Blogs: dedecole40.wordpress.com
Podcasts: Refinement Time (anchor.fm/randi-coley)
Social Media:
Facebook: www.facebook.com/Dedecole40
Instagram: CounselorsEscape
Youtube: Randi Coley

REFINEMENT TIME

In this heartfelt and unique poetry collection, the author navigates the labyrinth of human emotions, capturing moments of

love, loss, and resilience.

OVERCOMING

Overcoming: How I Stopped Living with Anxiety and Depression

It is a daily struggle to live life with the symptoms of anxiety and depression. Come on this journey with me as I work daily to overcome anxiety and depression...

www.ingramcontent.com/pod-product-compliance
Lightning Source LLC
Chambersburg PA
CBHW061323120626
46546CB00007B/2658